MAK

GETTING THE MOST OUT OF
MAKERSPACES
TO EXPLORE

MAR 2016

ARDUINO &
ELECTRONICS

DON RAUF

ROSEN
PUBLISHING
New York

Published in 2015 by The Rosen Publishing Group, Inc.
29 East 21st Street, New York, NY 10010

Library of Congress Cataloging-in-Publication Data

Rauf, Don, author.
Getting the most out of makerspaces to explore Arduino & electronics/Don Rauf.—First edition.
pages cm.—(Makerspaces)
Audience: Grades 5-8.
Includes bibliographical references and index.
ISBN 978-1-4777-7815-9 (library bound)—ISBN 978-1-4777-7817-3 (pbk.)—ISBN 978-1-4777-7818-0 (6-pack)
1. Arduino (Programmable controller)—Juvenile literature. 2. Arduino (Programmable controller)—Programming—Juvenile literature. 3. Electronics—Data processing—Juvenile literature. I. Title.
TJ223.P76R38 2015
629.8'955133—dc23
                                                                    2013048225

Manufactured in the United States of America

CONTENTS

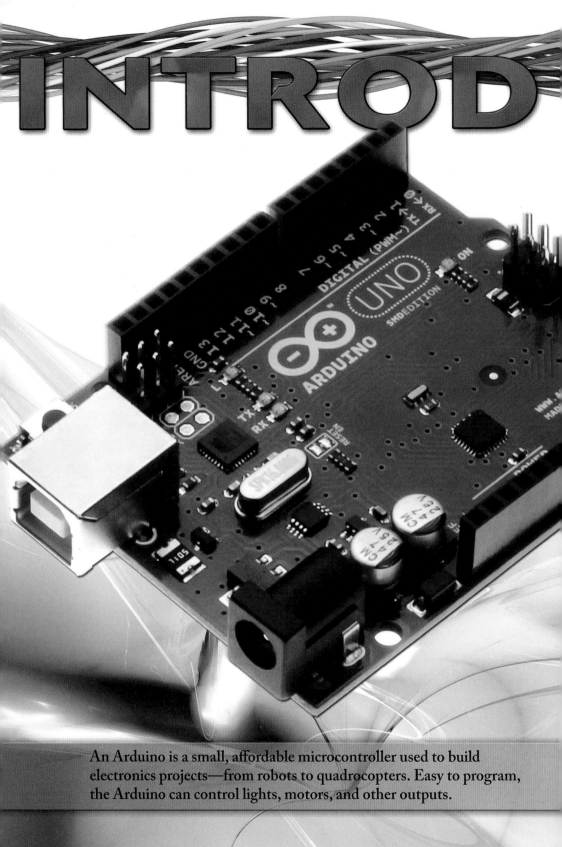

INTROD

An Arduino is a small, affordable microcontroller used to build electronics projects—from robots to quadrocopters. Easy to program, the Arduino can control lights, motors, and other outputs.

Makers are artists, engineers, hobbyists, enthusiasts, and students. They may also be amateurs interested in innovation and making new products for the community. Some makers go on to become entrepreneurs and even start their own companies. What is the maker movement, also known as makerspaces? Makerspaces are workshops that bring people together to do hands-on creative and often technology-oriented projects. They are teaching people to build robots, fix bicycles, program gadgets, make model airplanes, use 3-D printers, and more. The emphasis is on hands-on work and showing people that they can learn things that may at first seem beyond their grasp.

Makerspaces often take place in libraries or schools. They bring experts and beginners together to learn by doing and exploring. They provide a friendly, non-intimidating environment to create in. Makers are artists, hobbyists, enthusiasts, and students. They may also be amateurs interested in innovation and making new products for the community. Some makers go on to become entrepreneurs and even start their own companies.

Makerspaces have been friendly atmospheres for young people to learn all about electronics. Most people plug their devices into walls or power up their cell phones and laptops, yet they have no clue how these devices work. Arduino (pronounced ar-DWEE-no) is a new product that offers a fun way to learn about electronics, as well as computer programming, engineering, and possibly some robotics.

An Arduino is a microcontroller and does just what its name suggests. It is micro, or very small, and it is a controller, meaning it is a type of computer that can help a person control electronic gadgets. It's also affordable and easy to build. That's why it has been so popular in makerspaces. Those who have invented with it have come up with some wild ideas, such as making pocket pianos, remote-controlled lawn mowers, smartphone garage door openers, robots, and more. Most low-cost 3-D printers on the market today use Arduino-compatible microcontrollers.

This resource illustrates how makerspaces are allowing people to explore electronics and Arduino to empower them to dream up gadgets and other projects and make them come to life.

CHAPTER ONE

MAKING IDEAS COME TO LIFE

Want to make a coffee pot that sends a tweet when the coffee is ready? How about producing a cycling jacket with a flashing turn signal built in the back? Maybe making a fire-breathing animatronic pony is more your thing. How do you build one? The answer is Arduino.

Arduino has captured the imaginations of young people because it not only teaches programming and basic electronics but also shows how to put a program to immediate use in operating a real-life gadget. So what exactly is this magical thing called Arduino?

Arduino calls itself an "open-source electronics prototyping" platform based on flexible, easy-to-use hardware and software. Open-source means the program that operates Arduino is free, available for public use, and can be modified by anyone. Prototyping means that it allows you to make a first model of an idea or invention.

Arduino uses a low-cost microcontroller with a bunch of other user-friendly electronic components on a circuit board, which lets beginners and beyond create incredible things. An Arduino board plugs into all kinds of sensors, lights, motors, and other devices. It then easily combines with a simple software program that tells the device what to do. It's intended for artists, designers, hobbyists, and anyone interested in creating interactive objects or environments.

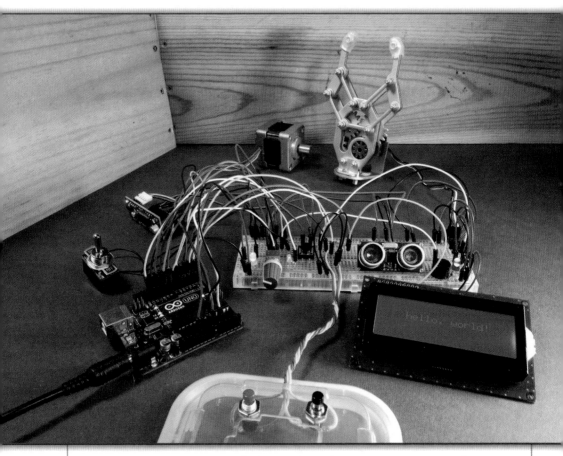

Many makerspaces use Arduino-based projects as an introduction to electronics and programming. The Arduino is easily wired to create interactive gadgets, toys, tools, and beyond.

If one goes online and searches for Arduino projects, many video clips of amazing and fun gadgets, toys, tools, and robots appear. One maker built an Arduino device that sends a Twitter message, or tweet, to his customers notifying them when fresh-baked goods have just come out of the oven. Another

Arduino project was electronic dice. With the push of a button, a random choice between one and six appears on an LED screen. A person can build a battery tester, a traffic light, and even a GPS system.

VIRTUAL MAKERSPACES CAMPS

Part of the fun of an Arduino makerspace project is collaborating with others to create. Sometimes, though, there may not be a makerspace project nearby. That's when those who want to start creating Arduino projects may turn to virtual "camps."

These camps are a series of online lessons presented over the course of several weeks. People either follow the camp on their own or get a group together and complete the activities. *Maker Magazine* hosts many of these events. It advertises free six-week virtual camps for anyone interested in DIY (do-it-yourself) projects. The goal is to have thirty days and thirty projects, and a new project is posted every day online.

The makerspace in the San Luis Obispo, California, library held a virtual maker camp one recent summer, inviting locals in to build Arduino-based creations and more. Search for virtual maker camps online and consider starting a program with local maker enthusiasts.

THE BIRTH OF ARDUINO

Massimo Banzi, who was an instructor at Interaction Design Institute Ivrea (IDII), came up with the idea for Arduino for his students in 2005 so that they could make their own electronics. He wanted them to be able to make electronics fast, and he wanted it to be affordable.

To get the project going, Banzi reached out to a colleague at the Massachusetts Institute of Technology (MIT) to develop a user-friendly programming language. He decided to make the software open-source so that it would be free for all to use. He and his collaborators also figured out how to make boards for about $30, a price that students could afford.

Banzi wanted his microprocessor board to stand out from the other boards on the market. The Arduino would be blue instead of the standard green, with a little image of his native Italy on the back. And unlike the other boards, it would have more input and output pins, or connections.

The Arduino board accepts and stores code from a computer so that a device can perform functions, like control light or play music. As David Cuartielles, one of the founding members said, the Arduino team wanted people to be able to learn and work with electronics from day one without having to learn algebra first.

When Banzi had figured out all the crucial elements, he put his newly born Arduino idea to the test. He and his collaborators supplied three hundred students with blank printed circuit boards. They gave them instructions on how to assemble them. Then the students had one task: create something with this new microcontroller board.

Massimo Banzi, a professor and electrical engineer, came up with the idea for Arduino and brought it to life with a team of four friends.

One of the first Arduino projects created by a student was an alarm clock that hung from the ceiling. Every time the user hit the snooze button, the clock would rise a little higher toward the ceiling, eventually forcing the person to stand up and get out of bed.

ARDUINO CATCHES ON FAST

Tom Igoe, a professor of physical computing at the Interactive Telecommunications Program at New York University, was so impressed with this user-friendly, affordable microcontroller

Arduino has branched out from its basic version to include a powerful Arduino Mega, a very small Arduino Nano, and a LilyPad Arduino *(pictured)*, which can be sewn into fabric.

that he became part of the core team. As Banzi said in *The Making of Arduino* by David Kushner, "We've enabled a lot of people to create products themselves."

Arduino is something physical (the hardware or tiny programmable computer that can make a gadget operate), an integrated development environment (where you enter, compile, and upload your code to the microcontroller board), and a programming language (the software that gives the instructions for the device to operate).

In the maker world, Arduino has caught on like wildfire, and Banzi and his team have been pressed to keep up with demand. They are now producing more than the original Arduino Uno boards. They have created a more powerful Arduino Mega, a compact Arduino Nano, an Internet-connectable Arduino Ethernet, and a waterproof LilyPad Arduino for clothing and e-textiles. Hundreds of thousands have been sold, and the movement is rapidly growing. Also, the more recent microprocessor-based Due and the upcoming Tre combine a microcontroller with a microprocessor. The Tre is being developed in partnership with the folks at BeagleBoard, makers of the BeagleBone.

CHAPTER TWO

ELECTRIFYING NEWS

For many who build Arduino projects, the format is their first introduction to using electricity. Arduino projects can run off of regular batteries or solar batteries, or be plugged into a wall socket (as long as an AC-to-DC converter is involved, but more on that later). Many experts call Arduino the friendliest way to learn about electronics. Many makerspaces, like the MENTOR makerspace at Lighthouse Community Charter School in Oakland, California, begin their sessions on Arduino with some simple lessons on electricity.

A current of electricity is a steady flow of electrons. For the electricity to bring power to any device, it needs a circuit. A circuit is a loop or pathway that electrons flow through. A lightbulb, for example, will have two wires attached to it so that electrons can travel to it and away from it in a circuit.

One can visualize this in real life by connecting a lightbulb to a battery. Online you can find this type of simple experiment. Attach one insulated wire from the negative end of a battery to a lightbulb. Attach another wire from the lightbulb to the positive end of the battery. As soon as the second wire touches the positive end of the battery, the circuit is complete. The bulb should light because electrons are flowing out of the negative terminal of the battery, through the bulb, and back into the positive side of the battery.

Arduino can be a great way to learn the basics of electronics. In makerspaces, young builders learn to solder and connect wires to make simple electronic circuits and components.

Before you plug into an Arduino, it's good to know some of the principles that have to do with electricity. Voltage is a measure of electrical potential measured in volts. Current is the amount of flow through a conductive material and is measured in amperes or amps. Resistance is opposition to electrical current and is measured in ohms. Voltage is usually abbreviated as V, resistance as R, and current as

I (from the French phrase *intensité de courant*, which is the same as current).

Measures of electricity all relate to something called Ohm's law, which says that voltage equals current times resistance. So the formula is V=IR. Say you have a 5-volt battery with positive and negative terminals, and a 100-ohm resistor is across it or in front of it in a circuit. To figure out current, you can use this formula, so $5 = I \times 100$, or current (I) = 5 ÷ 100 or .05 amps of current. This is how electricity is measured.

THE LAWS OF ELECTRICITY AND ARDUINO

How does Ohm's law apply to Arduino? Here's an example. Many Arduino projects use LEDs, or light emitting diodes. These are highly effective sources of light that are energy-efficient, using less power than traditional lightbulbs, and they last longer. Making LEDs light up is often a beginner Arduino project, and these lights can turn on with energy from a 5-volt battery.

Why not just connect a 5-volt battery directly to the LED without resistance? Why bother with the resistance? Why is it even part of the formula? Why not just send the power directly to the bulb? It's true that the LED will light up if connected directly to the battery because the diode allows any amount of current to flow through it. Without resistance, though, the LED will draw unlimited current from the source and drain

IF LIFE GIVES YOU LEMONS, MAKE ELECTRICITY

Arduino maintains a Web site that makes it easy to master some of the basics of electricity. A fun project that allows you to get a grasp of electricity fundamentals is to making a lemon into a power source. If you take a lemon and put a zinc nail and a copper penny into it, you have the beginnings of a power source. A lemon may even be able to power a low-voltage LED clock, although more than one lemon may be required.

The lemon juice serves as an electrolyte, in which charged atoms and molecules called ions dissolve and can flow over time. Since copper atoms attract electrons more than zinc atoms, electrons will pass from the zinc to the copper. Connect wires from the nail and penny to a small clock, and you may be able to generate enough power to have the clock telling time.

Potatoes and bananas may work in a similar way to generate power as well, and some Arduino enthusiasts have experiments using fruits and vegetables to power their Arduino. If you're ever trapped on a desert island, you might look for fruits and vegetables as an electricity source.

the battery very quickly. The LED may burn very brightly and get very hot. By creating resistance, the flow of electricity is turned down a bit, like closing a spigot a little so that the water runs slower. The resistor can make sure that proper current is reaching the LED. So resistors work to control current in an electric circuit by providing resistance. Again, in some ways, using a resistor is like closing off a tap on a water faucet so that the pressure is not as great.

AC/DC IS MORE THAN A HEAVY METAL BAND

The flow of electricity from a battery through a bulb and back is called direct current (DC). With DC power, the current flows in one direction. With alternate current (AC), current flows in opposite directions in regular cycles. AC current is the type of electricity used in homes and businesses throughout the world. We use AC electricity to power our televisions, lights, and computers. The regular back-and-forth motion of the electrons in a wire when powered by AC electricity is periodic motion, similar to that of a pendulum. AC is more popular because it is more suitable for long-distance transmission than DC electricity.

For the most part, Arduino uses DC current, and many projects can use a 5-volt battery to provide this DC charge. Arduino projects may be able to run off of AC current from a wall socket as long as it goes through a converter changing the current to DC first.

CHAPTER THREE

MAKING SPACE FOR AN ARDUINO MAKERSPACE

B ringing an Arduino project to life requires the right work environment. A person can't really set up a makerspace in a bedroom or at the kitchen table. As with any craft, hobby, or building project, having the right space and setup is crucial to being able to work effectively, and the same goes for an Arduino makerspace. With a name like "makerspace," it's clear that having the *space* is key.

SPACE EXPLORATION

A school may have a dedicated wood shop or auto shop with all the tools necessary to do makerspace-type work. Makerspaces, in many ways, borrow from technical and vocational education, and these shops often have tools that can help. Yet, if the tools aren't there, it shouldn't prevent anyone from getting a makerspace going. A room in a library, a workshop, or a computer lab in a school can all be potential makerspaces.

If you're a student who wants to start a makerspace, you might want to check with your school about how to secure a room. Some schools have art classes, home economics rooms, or photography classes that may be

Makerspaces are being set up in a variety of spaces, including computer labs, workshops, and community centers, as well as rooms in libraries and schools.

ideally suited to an Arduino maker project. In schools today, robotics clubs are growing, and Arduino is naturally suited for programming and operating small robots.

Outside of schools, people have started Arduino maker projects at 4-H Clubs, Girl Scouts, Boy Scouts, Boys & Girls Clubs, the YMCA and YWCA, community art centers, public libraries, museums, and science centers.

A makerspace can be temporary as well. These are sometimes called pop-ups. Makers and educators in Brooklyn, New York, got together and transformed an art gallery into a pop-up makerspace for kids. They outfitted the space with a 3-D printer called a MakerBot Replicator, a vinyl cutter, soldering equipment, electronics, and fabrication materials (these can be metal, plastic, or other materials).

Makerspace styles are going to vary with the amount of tools and materials they have. Some Arduino enthusiasts meet in rooms equipped with state-of-the-art technology, such as 3-D printers. However, an effective makerspace can also just be a room with empty tabletops and some access to electricity. Some groups meet in conference rooms in old libraries and make do with what they have. People can work with a minimal amount of tools and still accomplish amazing things.

The Makerspace.com Web site provides a manual called "The Makerspace Playbook," which offers guidelines to help people set up an effective makerspace or improve the work space they currently have for Arduino-based projects or other endeavors. The Makerspace Playbook is only a set of recommendations. Remember that makers and the spaces where they create can and do take many different forms.

TOOLS FOR ARDUINO

In addition to having a basic Arduino microprocessor board, some crucial tools are recommended for Arduino projects:

• A multimeter/oscilloscope is a meter that is helpful for checking voltages and continuity. Continuity shows if an electrical circuit is completely connected and able to conduct current.

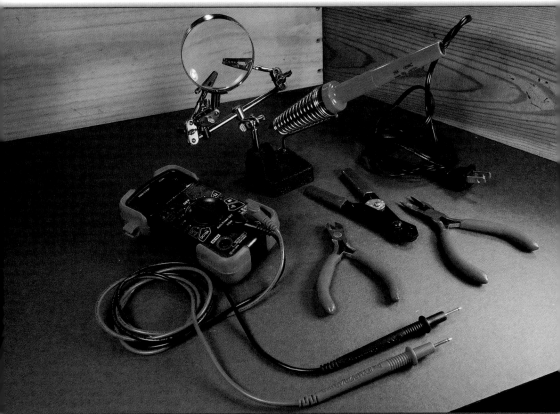

Building Arduino-based gadgets, devices, and robots requires the right tools, including wire cutters, wire strippers, a soldering iron, and a meter to check voltages and electrical current flow.

- Flush/diagonal cutters are the perfect tools for cutting wires and component leads.
- Wire strippers are needed to remove the insulation from the tip of a wire so that the wire can be connected to a component.
- A soldering iron is a tool that may be used for attaching wires and components to a circuit board. Hobbyists use one that looks like an electric pen and has a small screwdriver tip. It heats up to a point where it can melt a material called solder. Solder is an alloy (a mixture of metals) that is used to fuse electrical components together. Solder comes on a spool and looks like wire. It's another recommended supply to have on hand for building many Arduino projects.
- Needle-nose pliers are helpful for bending metal leads.
- A breadboard in case you don't have access to a soldering iron.

TIPS FOR MAKING A MAKERSPACE

These guidelines can help in establishing an effective area for making Arduino projects:

Make a space where projects can reside and not get harmed. If the woodshop in a school has room for an Arduino meetup, make sure the Arduino projects are safe from sawdust.

Make tools and materials visible. The spirit of makerspaces is in play and experimentation. When people can easily see the materials and tools they have to work with, it can help trig-

SAFETY FIRST

Makers have to be careful not to harm themselves or others. Always have a first-aid kit that is readily accessible and a means to call 911 in case of emergencies.

The electricity used for Arduino work is generally safe. Most electronic circuits use low voltages—for example, the 5 to 12 volts needed to power any Arduino projects. Arduinos can be powered by batteries or external plug-in transformers. Transformers convert the voltage to a safe level that will make the electronic circuit work. Also, in most cases, transformers convert the signal from AC (as supplied from the wall socket) to DC (used for most electronic circuits). Like batteries, these transformers are safe to use. They are typically double-insulated, and no high-voltage parts are accessible to a user.

ger new ideas. Can tools be hung on the wall? Can containers be provided to accommodate a variety of materials—plastics, wood, metal, lights, buttons, wires, and more? Participants want to be able to sift through and explore to get ideas. Space to store projects is also ideal.

For sources of inspiration, some Arduino makerspaces keep newspaper and magazine clippings on hand of other Arduino projects so that members can be inspired by what others have done. A makerspace encourages individuals to bring in gadgets, toys, and other items that will fuel new thoughts, directions, and innovation. Shelves and wall space to display all can help.

Have enough room on a worktable. Arduino makers need to start with a clean slate—usually a clean empty table where they can lay out their components and tools and get their work done. Being neat and organized at a worktable helps in following instructions and completing tasks.

Togetherness and separateness are key. Ideally, an Arduino makerspace is an area where people can come together and share and communicate. However, it is also a space where people can work on their own so that they can build and tinker.

Have a source of electricity. Depending on what a person builds, a source of electricity may be needed. Hooking up an LCD display to Arduino could require some soldering.

Think of the mess. Makers need room to get messy, but they also have to be able to clean up when they are done. Have all the means for cleaning up and disposing of waste materials at the ready.

Provide Internet access. An easy, fast way to connect to Web sites can be very helpful as questions come up while building a project.

CHAPTER FOUR

ARDUINO OUT OF THE BOX

Massimo Banzi, the creator of Arduino, has said that you don't need someone's permission to create something great. Arduino gives the tools to do just that. We know that Arduino is a small computer that one can program to read and control electrical components. But where do you find all the pieces necessary to really start building something in Arduino?

The Arduino microcontroller is attached to a circuit board, which is an insulated board on which interconnected circuits and components are mounted or etched. To get an Arduino, go online and start to shop around. The official Arduino Web site gives a full listing of distributors that sell Arduino kits and related supplies. Adafruit, SparkFun Electronics, and Maker Shed are a few of the more popular sites where you can purchase such components. There are things such as Arduino clones as well. These are copies of the true Arduino projects and are worth checking out.

On sites like those mentioned above, the basic Arduino Uno runs about $30. Some makerspace groups may conduct a learning session and ask that all members purchase an Arduino starter kit, which can cost between $65 and $85. A kit may give you LEDs, transistors, motors, integrated circuits, pushbuttons, variable resistors, photo resistors, temperature sensors, and relays. An experimenter's guide shows how to use

An Arduino has many pins where wires connect and either take information in or transmit information or instructions out to perform a function.

all the pieces and start building projects. A local electronics shop, such as RadioShack, may sell Arduino as well.

GET TO KNOW YOUR ARDUINO

A notable feature of an Arduino is its many pins or connecting points that can be set up as inputs or outputs. Examples of inputs are a temperature sensor, a motion sensor, and a distance sensor or switch. These devices feed information into the computer. Examples of outputs would be a light, a screen, or a motor. The computer sends information out to these devices on how to operate.

Arduinos let makers write code and construct devices that interact with the world around them through sensors that respond to light, temperature, voice, motion, and other types of input.

Most projects with Arduino require having a USB A-to-B cable. A starter kit most likely has this, and many people may have one with their computers at home. The cable is key when it comes to transferring a program written on a computer to the Arduino board.

An Arduino board has a little light in its lower-left corner. When the USB cord is plugged in, this light may flash. When downloading a program from a computer, the Arduino may be powered from this USB connection. Once the USB is disconnected, the Arduino will need to be powered from a different energy supply through its power jack. The external power supply can either be from an AC-to-DC adapter or a battery. The adapter can plug into a port on the Arduino and a battery can connect via leads from a battery that are inserted in the "Gnd" and "Vin" pin headers of the POWER connector. Gnd is a ground pin, and Vin is the input voltage to the board from an external source. Ground pins complete the circuit.

PROGRAMMING THE DEVICE

To tell any Arduino gizmo what to do, programming is required. An Arduino software package that matches your operating system (Windows, Mac OS X, and Linux) can be found on the Arduino download page. The programming language is free and adaptable. Write the code and upload it to the Arduino board. The code a person writes for Arduino is known as sketches and the language is C++. Make sure that Arduino is installed in a computer that will be used to program Arduino projects.

When you connect things like lights and sensors to the Arduino, they plug into the pins and a maker has to keep careful track of where things are plugged in. This is vital information for the program. If there is a light on the board connected to pin 13, for example, the program will indicate the pin location and then identify it as an output. With simple programming instructions, the user can turn the light on and then turn the light off. Another simple program can have the light turning on and off at intervals so that it appears to be blinking.

USING A BREADBOARD (NOT FOR SLICING BREAD)

Many Arduino projects also begin on something called a breadboard, sometimes called a protoboard because the board is used for prototyping a project. This means one can make a temporary layout of a circuit on the board without any required soldering. It is a rectangular plastic box filled with holes. Poke jumper wires though the holes and they connect with lines of metal that connect rows and columns to make circuits. The metal is constructed in such a way that when a wire is poked through the hole, the metal underneath the hole grabs onto it.

The breadboards are easily changeable and reusable. Typically, makers use the breadboard to make sure everything

WIRED UP

Almost all Arduino projects require wiring. For about $6, a pack of seventy-five jumper wires can be purchased. They are made of copper surrounded by a plastic insulator. Wires make circuits and allow all pieces to communicate. They transfer electrical signals to the microcontroller.

They can vary in size and sometimes in color to help creators better identify their purpose. Depending on the wire used, it may have to be stripped of its coating at the tips to expose the metal part.

works right before making an item permanent. Then, when everything is correct, it can be saved in a permanent version.

MAKING IT PERMANENT

When a project is ready to be made permanent, a maker may shift it all over to a printed circuit board (PCB) or Veroboard (stripboard). A printed circuit board is sturdier than a breadboard. Wires and components can be soldered in place.

A Veroboard is somewhere in between a solder-less breadboard and a PCB. It allows you to make a more permanent circuit, which has more reliable connections than a breadboard, but without the time and expense of creating a PCB. Making a PCB can be an involved process, but go online and there are several lessons on how to make a cheap, easy, and fast PCB.

There are universal PCBs that have rows of individual holes throughout the board and metal lines connecting the holes in each row, much like the breadboard. Parts and wires can be mounted on the face of the board. Wires and elements can be soldered in place. Whether it's a printed circuit board or a Veroboard, these options can make a gadget or system made from Arduino last a very long time.

CHAPTER FIVE

Imagine It, Build It: A Simple Arduino Project

Now that you know some of the fundamentals of Arduino, you can move on and actually start to take your ideas and bring them to life. To take the first step into building something with Arduino, try to make blinking lights. This process lets one become familiar with the foundation of how to create with Arduino.

Getting started on this requires an Arduino, a USB cable, wires, and a breadboard. Because this exercise is about lights, get about five small LED lights. This is all the hardware you'll need. Software is necessary as well—the program that will tell the lights what to do.

Generally, small LEDs will have two wire "legs" coming out of the bottom of them. One is longer than the other. The shorter leg connects to the ground and the longer leg connects to the positive voltage source. For example, if there are five LED lights to be lit, the legs of the lights have to be properly positioned so that the longer legs are in the breadboard holes for positive energy and the shorter ones are into ground. Each light will have its own black wire for ground, but one master black wire for ground will feed from a dedicated negative row on the breadboard to the Arduino.

After ground wires are in place, put a different color wire in the same column as the long leg for each light.

Many Arduino beginners start by making a simple lighting project using LEDs (light emitting diodes) and a breadboard, which is a platform for making an adjustable circuit layout.

Each color wire will be connected to the positive source of energy. The black wire connects to the pin labeled "GND" for ground, and then each color wire connects to a numbered pin on the Arduino—each is a positive energy source. For example, the wires can connect to pin #12, #11, #10, #9, and #8. This is a complete hardware setup.

GET TOGETHER: HOW TO FIND OR START AN ARDUINO MEETUP

To make more advanced projects with Arduino, collaborating can help, and that, of course, is what makerspaces are for. Try to find makerspaces that already exist and are dedicated to Arduino. You can also try to set up your own Arduino maker-space, but another option is to search for an Arduino meetup in your area. Meetups are groups of people with shared interests who plan meetings and form offline clubs in local communities. If you search for Arduino meetups, more than four hundred groups around the world are listed with more than seventy-three thousand members. It's not unusual for makerspaces and meetups to overlap, and many meetups have brought like-minded people together who go on to form makerspaces.

GET A PROGRAM RUNNING

With hardware ready, a maker turns to the program. The goal is to have each light turn on and off in a row, so the first light goes on and off, then the second, etc. This action is to repeat continuously. The program can tell the Arduino to do exactly that.

Code that the maker writes can loop repeatedly. In this case, the loop will turn the LEDs on and off continuously. The code in the program identifies pins 8 through 12 as output pins because information from the computer program will be causing an action outside of the computer. The maker then writes a line of code identifying the pin by number and setting the mode to "High." At "High," the Arduino is sending out 5 volts and turning on the light. To keep the light on for a second, a line of code indicating a delay is needed. Try delay (1,000). This means 1,000 milliseconds, and it will tell the program to wait one second before going on to the next step in the code.

After the delay, a line of code is needed that tells the light to turn off. This requires writing in the word "Low," which signals that zero voltage should run to the light. Again, the maker writes instructions so that the light will stay on a second and then stay turned off a second. Then the maker writes instructions for the next light in the series, identifying that LED by the pin number to which it is connected. Overall the maker in this project is writing code that tells each light to turn on for a second and then turn off for a second. Once code like that is written for each light, the program can be set up to repeat.

The written program in Arduino is called a sketch. When the sketch is complete, it needs to be uploaded into the Arduino via the USB cable. It's as simple as hitting the upload button on the computer screen. Once the program is uploaded, it begins, and the lights should begin blinking—turning on and off, one after the other.

PUTTING ON THE FINAL TOUCHES

The program can be adjusted, too. Make the lights blink faster by shortening the delay time. Change delay (1,000) to delay (500), and the lights will turn on and off every half second instead of every second.

This is a very beginning exercise to start with to learn Arduino. One of the attractive features of Arduino, however, is that it can operate a gadget using sensory information. Sensors that detect light, sound, and temperature can be incorporated into a device and react. A robot, for example, can detect heat or light with sensors, and move toward heat or light. Arduino programs can also control lights, buttons, and switches. One of the best ways to learn is to find an Arduino makerspace and learn with others.

Another great thing to keep in mind as projects get more advanced is that makers often offer their code already written for free online. People store their code and programs for Arduino in "libraries." Libraries allow other people to easily use the code that you've written and update it as you improve the library.

CHAPTER SIX

THE WIDE WORLD OF ARDUINO PROJECTS

In the last chapter, we explored the basics of how to program Arduino to make LEDs blink. On the Web, many lessons are offered that help build Arduino skills step by step. Here are some starter projects with Arduino:

Electronic dice: Instead of rolling physical dice, an Arduino can be programmed to choose random numbers between one and six. With a push of a button, two random numbers can appear on a screen. It can add an extra element of fun to that next game of Monopoly.

Super simple strobe: The Arduino is always easy to use as a light control. A great site to get started with a few simple projects is Sylvia's Super-Awesome Maker Show. This site, like many others, provides the code already written, so it's just a matter of cutting and pasting when it comes to putting code in place to run the program. A strobe light project can create a fun environment—a strobe can make moving objects look like they are motionless.

A talking clock: On a Web site called Chlonos, directions are given on how to build an open-source talking multimedia clock gadget, or, simply, a talking clock. This is more sophisticated than some projects and involves a speech engine, which is a speech synthesizer,

Arduino enthusiasts have made some fun yet simple creations, including strobe lights, talking clocks, secret-knock locks for doors, and electronic dice.

plus various analog sensors and audio circuits. A video on the site takes the viewer through the step-by-step process for building it.

A "**plantuino:**" This was the name given to a greenhouse using Arduino and sensors that relay if the ground is wet or dry. When the ground is dry, the Arduino, which is connected to a hose, turns on the watering system. When it is wet, it turns off.

A **secret-knock lock:** An ingenious device with Arduino as the brains allows the user to program in a rhythm that triggers a small motor to activate and open a door lock. Imagine rapping on a door with a secret knock and a door opens, almost as if by magic.

A **jacket with directional lights:** The LilyPad Arduino is a microcontroller board designed for wearables and e-textiles (fabrics that enable digital or electronic components). It can be sewn into fabric (like a sweatshirt) with conductive thread (which is a way to connect various electronics onto clothing). Using this type of Arduino, one maker created a bicycling jacket with directional signals on the back. Push a button on the left cuff near the wrist and it indicates a left turn signal. Push a button on the right cuff near the wrist and it indicates a right turn signal. It's perfect for the bicyclist who needs to be seen at night.

A bubble machine: One maker online made a "Bubbles-teen Bubble Machine," which may be named so because it looks cobbled together in a Frankenstein-like manner. Here again, Arduino gets combined with servo motors. One motor operates a device that dips a wand into bubble solution. Another motor operates a fan that turns on to blow the bubbles.

MOTORIZE IT

Arduinos can work together with motors to perform advanced functions. Servo motors are commonly used because they are small. They have been used in toy cars, robots, and airplanes. They're energy-efficient, and they can be operated by remote control or radio control.

Arduino makers have put servo motors to some crazy uses. One maker created an Arduino that could sense when laces on a sneaker were becoming loose. Then the motors would kick in and pull the laces tighter.

Many makerspaces offer programs in building robots, and Arduino just recently introduced Arduino Robot, which is

MY ARDUINO JUST TWEETED ME!

Can an Arduino really send a tweet? It's true. An Arduino may be more able to use social networking tools than some humans you know. One project on the Internet demonstrates how an Arduino-based gadget can be programmed to read temperature and humidity in a room and then send a tweet at regular intervals with that information. An affordable component called an Ethernet Shield costs about $10 and gives Internet connectivity to a basic Arduino. According to technology writer Darren Yates, it's "dead easy" to program.

A company called Botanicalls has an Arduino-based kit that connects to plants in a home. When soil is dry, a moisture detector triggers the Arduino to send a tweet to a phone: "Your plant needs watering!" Another project lets the maker make a pot of coffee via Twitter. With the right setup, a coffee lover can be on the bus and send a tweet to the coffee pot at home, starting the pot so that fresh java is waiting when he or she walks through the door.

One tinkerer in *Make Magazine* presented his Kitty Twitty Cat Toy that sends tweets to the owner, showing that the cat is playing. The toy has the potential to be triggered by tweet as well—vibrating and moving around the room so that an owner can play with his or her cat from the office via Twitter.

the first official Arduino on wheels. Schools often offer extracurricular programs dedicated to robots as well, and many of these classes work with Arduino. Robots combine many elements that show advanced uses of Adruino—motors, light displays, heat sensors, light sensors, and more. Why are robots popular? Because they can be both fun and functional. Who doesn't want a robot to do his or her bidding?

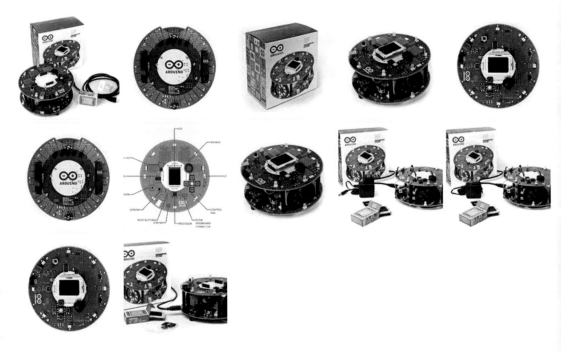

A relatively new version of Arduino called Arduino Robot *(pictured here)* is a tiny computer on wheels specifically designed to make a robot that will perform all sorts of tasks.

Popular Mechanics gives instructions on how to build a first robot. It's centered around Arduino and estimated to cost only about $100. The microcontroller on this project is powered by a 9-volt battery. This bot uses two servo gear motors for propulsion.

Web sites feature a few simple lesson plans where an Arduino is attached to a breadboard, motors, wheels,

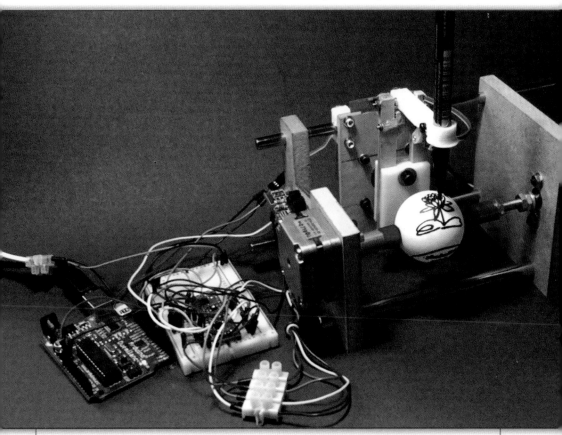

If you find robotics intriguing, you may want to look into egg-botics. A popular Arduino-based contraption is the Eggbot, which draws designs and messages on eggs and egg-shaped items.

batteries, and a few other components. The Web site Community of Robots is a good place to start. Note that the Arduino needs batteries for power, but so do the motors.

After mastering a basic robot, makers often go on to build robots with specific functions, such as soda-serving robots, floor-cleaning robots, and plant-watering robots. Instructables.com shows how to build a chess-playing robot, a tree-climbing robot, and a fire-breathing animatronic pony.

Some makers have basically robotized their lawnmowers so that they can control them by remote. Instead of pushing the lawnmower around the yard, a person can sit back in a lawn chair and guide a lawn mower around the yard, moving forward and backward, and getting the job done without breaking a sweat.

Also check out the Eggbot. Eggbots are basically art robots that can draw elaborate patterns on spherical or egg-shaped objects. There are many types of Eggbots shown on the Internet, and some are powered by Arduino. They are top-sellers for many electronics companies, so go online and see what all the fuss is about. It may inspire you to enter the world of egg-botics.

CHAPTER SEVEN

ARDUINO ON THE MOVE

Corporate America is quickly noticing that the maker movement is producing technological talent of the future. Microchip maker Intel has recognized the innovation of Arduino. The company recently unveiled the Intel Galileo board, the first product in a new family of Arduino-compatible development boards featuring Intel architecture. The company recently donated fifty thousand Arduino-compatible microcontroller boards to one thousand universities. Arduino has also partnered with semiconductor maker Texas Instruments in developing a more powerful version of the Arduino.

RadioShack has also jumped aboard the Arduino bandwagon. The electronics retail giant not only sells the product, but it also holds an Arduino competition, seeking the project that best shows how to use Arduino in an innovative way. Companies are sponsoring makerspaces as well. Pacific Gas & Electric, Botball Robotics, ING, and Lowes all have programs that can help fund makerspaces.

Arduino is now a tool used by many museums. In a March 16, 2011, *New York Times* article, Nick Bilton called it "the driving force behind most of the interactive exhibits seen in museums and galleries today." Arduino allows the museum-goer to touch a button and hear prerecorded background material or light up an artwork.

This time-lapse camera dolly won RadioShack's Great Create Arduino Challenge for maker Jay Miley.

The museum technology Web site Openexhibits.org says that some of the types of interactivity a museum can build with Arduino include:

- A DJ mixing board exhibit with controls that allow multiple users to combine, distort, and remix audio clips
- An exhibit about nutrition where miniature replicas of different foods can be sorted on a screen into their correct food groups

EMPOWERING YOUNG WOMEN

One of the great things about the maker movement is that it's brought both young men and women into the worlds of engineering and programming. With her shocking pink hair, Limor Fried, age thirty-three, is a spokeswoman for the maker movement. In fact, some call her the queen of the maker movement. She has become a champion to young women, showing that women can grasp engineering, electronics, computer programming, and innovation.

Fried is the founder of Adafruit Industries, an electronics hobbyist company, and she goes by the name of LadyAda. (The name pays homage to Augusta Ada King, a nineteenth-century mathematician and a programmer of an early computer.)

Started in her college dorm room at MIT, Adafruit offers a wide variety of free electronic tutorials and forums for makers, including lessons on Arduino from the beginner level to more advanced. Adafruit sells hardware, like Arduino kits, that run on open-source software. Fried's most popular invention is MintyBoost—she took a tin of the breath fresheners Altoids, crammed it with batteries, and enabled it to be used to recharge a phone or an MP3 player. She encourages the sharing of technology. In seven years, her company has grown to twenty-five employees and is now a multimillion-dollar business.

Limor Fried of Adafruit is a huge supporter of Arduino and encourages women to get involved in the maker movement. Here, she is speaking onstage with John Briggs at TechCrunch.

Recently, *Entrepreneur* magazine named her Entrepreneur of the Year.

Fried is fiercely dedicated to teaching young people about the rewards and fun of engineering and science. She was fascinated with the way things work from a young age. In third grade, she took apart her VCR to see how it worked. At MIT, where she studied engineering, she created a device that disabled all cell phones in her immediate vicinity—she got fed up with people yammering all the time on their cell phones and she figured out a way to make them stop with a push of a button. Fried hopes other young women will take inspiration from her.

- An exhibit that explains how mechanical clocks work with multiple controls like levers and switches to speed, slow, or change the timing mechanism
- A virtual chess exhibit that allows visitors to play

Museums are really institutions dedicated to creating in the first place, so it makes sense that they've embraced Arduino, a tool of the maker movement. Plus, museums are opening their own makerspaces. Newark Museum, Omaha Children's Museum, Children's Museum of Pittsburgh, and many others now have makerspaces.

ADVANCEMENTS THROUGH ARDUINO

The more Arduino has spread, the more uses have been discovered for the microcontroller. Arduino's uses may now be advancing into the world of health and medicine. An Akron, Ohio, teenager has used it to build the Arduino Powered Personal Limb Exerciser (APPLE). Joseph Anand had an interest in helping veterans. He programmed the Arduino to control a small motor that attaches to a limb in need of physical therapy. He then programmed a Microsoft Kinect game console to administer a doctor-approved physical therapy regimen. Anand is a huge fan of the maker movement, and he recently presented his innovation to more than seventy thousand visitors at the Maker Faire at the New York Hall of Science.

CHAPTER EIGHT

BEYOND ARDUINO

Certainly Arduino is a great introduction to using programming to make physical things operate. But electronic tinkerers in makerspaces may want to go a step beyond and try other microcontrollers. Arduino may have many advantages because it's open-source, easy to work with, and requires very little energy to operate.

HOW ABOUT SOME RASPBERRY PI?

Raspberry Pi is a small and affordable microcontroller kit that sells for about $35. It operates on Linux (a free and open-source operating system). Raspberry Pi features two USB ports and an HDMI (high-definition multimedia interface) output. This is one of the best ways to transmit audio and video for a home theater or other viewing screen. It operates like a mini computer. It's easy to plug into a television and a mouse. A keyboard can even be attached to it to operate it like a regular computer.

Raspberry Pi also features an Ethernet port, so it can access the Internet readily. Makers mostly use it for projects that require a graphic interface or a strong Internet connection. Many makerspaces devote sessions to building projects with Raspberry

Pi, and the Raspberry Pi Web site provides some fun ideas to get started.

GOOD TO THE BONE?

Another microcontroller is called BeagleBone, and some techies describe it as a combination of Arduino and Rasp-

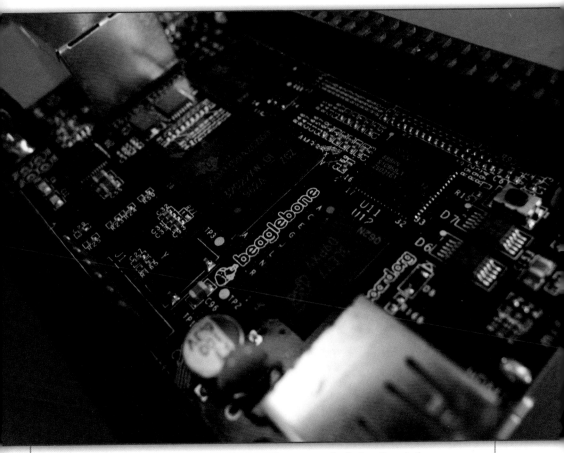

BeagleBone is a microcontroller similar to an Arduino but is known for its power and ninety-two possible connection points. Raspberry Pi is another small platform that can make gadgets operate.

berry Pi. The BeagleBone Black is thought to be a little more difficult to learn, but it can be used for more advance projects. Still, like Pi and Arduino, it gives makers, artists, and engineers the ability to create original projects.

BeagleBone has ninety-two possible connection points and a great range of interface options, while Arduino has fourteen input/output pins. The BeagleBone is fast. When it comes to showing video streams, Raspberry Pi may beat all in terms of showing the graphics, but BeagleBone is powerful.

Because it is relatively new on the scene, it may be hard to find makerspace programs devoted to the product, but its popularity is growing.

THE FUTURE OF MAKERSPACES

Some people believe that makerspaces may spawn the next industrial revolution. The movement is encouraging young people to embrace technology and come up with new projects that they can build themselves. While most makerspaces are community-based groups, some for-profit businesses are now opening based on the makerspace model, such as California's TechShop, which is a makerspace chain, and FabLab. These new types of makerspaces invite anyone with an idea to join, create, make stuff, and possibly get some technical training—for a membership fee. Companies like the automaker Ford have begun funding employees' makerspace memberships because they see that innovation may come from this type of environment. The

OTHER MICROCONTROLLERS

Another type of microcontroller to look into is the Parallax Propellor. A recent contest looking for the next generation in medical innovation called upon makerspace groups to use microcontrollers and sensors to create open-source medical applications and products for possible use in the health care industry. Free contest kits were given away containing the Parallax Propeller.

Arduino actually uses what's called an AVR microcontroller, and some makers use just an AVR microcontroller for projects instead of the Arduino system. An AVR on its own can be much smaller than an Arduino, which can have advantages for certain projects.

Meanwhile, Arduino itself is advancing and making more versions of the Arduino so that users don't have to buy add-ons—for example, the Arduino Yun. *Yun* means "cloud" in Chinese, and this new Arduino can access the Internet with great ease.

belief is that real innovation and change can come from tinkering.

A young man from Seattle once took a do-it-yourself approach with computers. He ordered a mini-computer

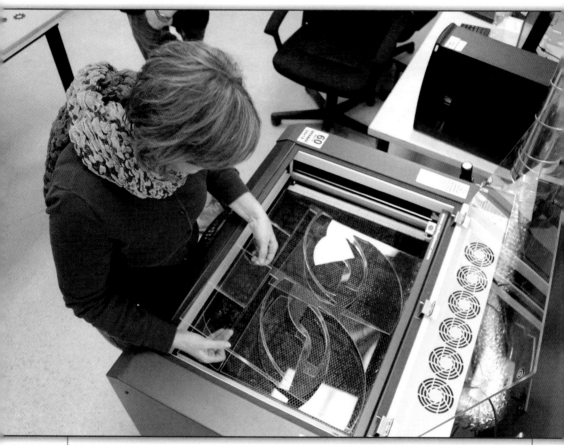

Many makerspaces today are equipped with cutting-edge technology, such as 3-D printers and laser cutters. With these modern tools, young makers have the opportunity to bring their ideas to life.

from *Popular Mechanics* and rewrote its software. His interest in creating with new technology paid off. That young man was Bill Gates, and he formed one of the most successful companies of all time—Microsoft. So explore a makerspace near you. You never know where the experience may lead.

alternating current (AC) This is the most common type of electrical power in the world. Electrons in AC current move one direction for 1/60th of a second, and then go the other direction for 1/60th of a second.

breadboard Also called a "protoboard," this is a base for prototyping electronics and circuits. Elements are easily changed and moved on a breadboard.

circuit A pathway through which electrical current flows. The path starts and ends at the same point. Electronic circuits tend to be low voltage.

conductor A material that lets electrons or electricity move easily through it. Wiring is often made of copper, and high-voltage cables are often made of aluminum.

current The flow rate of electrons through a circuit, measured in amps.

direct current (DC) An electric current that flows continuously in one direction.

insulator A material through which electrons and electricity cannot flow. Glass and plastics are good insulators.

light emitting diode (LED) An electronic device that emits light when an electrical current passes through it.

loop A fundamental programming idea where a sequence of instructions is continuously repeated.

microcontroller A compact computer that may operate a system in a robot, motor vehicle, office machine, medical device, vending machine, home appliance, or other devices.

ohm A measure of resistance to electrical current.

Ohm's law A formula used to calculate the right voltage, current, and resistance for a circuit. The formula is voltage equals current times resistance, or V = IR. Current is abbreviated with an "I."

open-source A computer program that provides free access to source code for the general public to use and even modify its original design.

pin The input and output point on an Arduino device.

prototype An original or first model of something from which other forms are copied or developed.

resistor An electrical component that provides resistance against the voltage. It acts like a control to regulate the flow of electricity.

sketch The name that Arduino uses for a program. It's the unit of code that is uploaded to the Arduino to tell it what to do.

3-D printing A manufacturing process that builds physical objects layer by layer by a high-tech, computer-controlled device.

voltage A measure of electrical force, which can be described as the push or pressure of the electrons through a circuit.

Association of Information Technology Professionals (AITP)
330 N. Wabash Avenue, Suite 2000
Chicago, IL 60611-4267
Web site: http://www.aitp.org
(800) 224-9371
This worldwide society of professionals in information technology offers career training, scholarships, news, and social networking opportunities.

Canadian Advanced Technology Alliance (CATA)
207 Bank Street, Suite 416
Ottawa, ON K2P 2N2
Canada
(613) 236-6550
Web site: http://www.cata.ca
The largest high-tech association in Canada, the CATA is a comprehensive resource of latest high-tech news in Canada.

Canadian Association for the Advancement of Science (CAAS)
P.O. Box 75513
3034 Edgemont Boulevard
North Vancouver, BC V7R 4X1
Canada
Web site: http://caas-acascience.org
This organization encourages Canadians of all ages to explore ideas and information regarding science and technology. The group's goal is to help people learn about science and its

impact on their lives and make connections between science, technology, and their society. The CAAS organizes many youth programs.

Consumer Electronics Association
1919 S. Eads Street
Arlington, VA 22202
(866) 858-1555
Web site: http://www.ce.org
This professional group offers news on technology trends and the latest in consumer electronic products.

National Association of Programmers (NAP)
P.O. Box 529
Prairieville, LA 70769
Web site: http://www.napusa.org
This group is dedicated to providing information and resources to help programmers, developers, consultants, and students in the computer industry.

WEB SITES

Due to the changing nature of Internet links, Rosen Publishing has developed an online list of Web sites related to the subject of this book. This site is updated regularly. Please use this link to access the list:

http://www.rosenlinks.com/MAKER/Ardu

Banzi, Massimo. *Getting Started with Arduino* (Make: Projects). Sebastapol, CA: O'Reilly Media, 2009.

Boxall, John. *Arduino Workshop: A Hands-On Introduction with 65 Projects*. San Francisco, CA: No Starch Press, 2013.

Brennan, Patricia. *Who Is Bill Gates?* New York, NY: Grosset & Dunlap, 2013.

Farrell, Mary. *Computer Programming for Teens*. Boston, MA: Thomas Course Technology, 2008.

Ford, Jerry Lee. *Programming for the Absolute Beginner* (No Experience Required). Boston, MA: Thomson Course Technology, 2007.

Freedman, Jeri. *Careers in Computer Science and Programming*. New York, NY: Rosen Classroom, 2011.

Goldsworthy, Steve. *Steve Jobs* (Remarkable People). New York, NY: Av2 by Weigl, 2011.

Grant, Michael. *BZRK*. New York, NY: Egmont, 2012.

Lusted, Marcia Amidon. *Mark Zuckerberg: Facebook Creator* (Essential Lives). Edina, MN: ABDO Publishing, 2012.

Margolis, Michael. *The Arduino Cookbook*. Sebastapol, CA: O'Reilly Media, 2011.

Marques, Marcelo. *Hackerteen: Volume 1: Internet Blackout*. Sebastopol, CA: O'Reilly Media, 2009.

McRoberts, Michael. *Beginning Arduino*. New York, NY: Apress, 2010.

Monk, Simon. *Arduino + Android Projects for the Evil Genius: Control Arduino with Your Smartphone or Tablet*. New York, NY: McGraw-Hill/TAB Electronics, 2011.

Monk, Simon. *Programming Arduino: Getting Started with Sketches*. New York, NY: McGraw-Hill/TAB Electronics, 2011.

Monk, Simon. *30 Arduino Projects for the Evil Genius*. New York, NY: McGraw-Hill/TAB Electronics, 2010.

Nussey, John. *Arduino for Dummies*. Hoboken, NJ: Wiley Publishing, 2013.

Oxer, Jonathan, and Hugh Blemings. *Practical Arduino: Cool Projects for Open Source Hardware*. New York, NY: Apress, 2009.

Sande, Warren, and Carter Sande. *Hello World! Computer Programming for Kids and Other Beginners*. Greenwich, CT: Manning, 2009.

Sethi, Maneesh. *Game Programming for Teens*. Boston, MA: Thomson Course Technology, 2009.

Warren, John-David, Josh Adams, and Harold Malle. *Arduino Robotics*. New York, NY: Apress, 2011.

Bilton, Nick. "An Interactive Exhibit for About $30." *New York Times*, March 16, 2011. Retrieved November 25, 2013 (http://www.nytimes.com).

Chalkley, Andrew. "The Absolute Beginner's Guide to Arduino." January 1, 2013. Retrieved November 25, 2013 (http://forefront.io/a/beginners-guide-to-arduino).

Hayward, David. "25 Fun Things to Do with a Raspberry Pi." CNET, November 28, 2012. Retrieved November 25, 2013 (http://reviews.cnet.co.uk/desktops/25-fun-things-to-do-with-a-raspberry-pi-50009851).

Instructables. "Arduino Electronics 101." Retrieved November 25, 2013 (http://www.instructables.com/id/Arduino-Electronics-101).

Instructables. "20 Unbelievable Arduino Projects." Retrieved November 25, 2013 (http://www.instructables.com/id/20-Unbelievable-Arduino-Projects).

Klosowski, Daniel. "How to Pick the Right Electronics Board for Your DIY Project." Lifehacker, July 11, 2013. Retrieved November 25, 2013 (http://lifehacker.com).

Kushner, David. "The Making of Arduino." IEEE Spectrum, October 26, 2011. Retrieved November 25, 2013 (http://spectrum.ieee.org/geek-life/hands-on/the-making-of-arduino/0).

Ladyada.net. "Arduino Tutorial." Retrieved November 25, 2013 (http://www.ladyada.net/learn/arduino).

Maker Camp. "Free Virtual DIY Camp for Teens: Cool Projects, Epic Field Trips & Awesome Makers." Retrieved November 25, 2013 (http://www.makezine.com/maker-camp).

Makerspace. "Places." Retrieved November 25, 2013 (http://www.makerspace.com/places).

MITVideo. "Arduino Tutorial #1." Retrieved November 25, 2013 (http://video.mit.edu/watch/arduino-tutorial-1-10950).

Olivetti. "Olivetti: A Story of Innovation and Growth." Retrieved November 25, 2013 (http://www.olivetti.nu/history.htm).

Processing 2. "Download Processing/Play with Examples." Retrieved November 25, 2013 (http://www.processing.org).

StackExchange. "How Do I Go from Arduino Breadboard to Creating a Real Device?" Retrieved May 11, 2011 (http://electronics.stackexchange.com/questions/14146/how-do-i-go-from-arduino-breadboard-to-creating-a-real-device).

Sylvia's Super-Awesome Maker Show. "Super Simple Adjustable Strobe for Arduino." August 30, 2010. Retrieved November 25, 2013 (http://www.sylviashow.com/strobe).

TechHive. "Geek 101: What Is Arduino?" Retrieved November 25, 2013 (http://www.techhive.com/article/239454/geek_101_what_is_arduino.html).

Teconomy. "Can the Maker Movement Re-Make America?" September 17, 2013. Retrieved November 25, 2013 (http://www.teconomy.com).

WikiHow. "How to Make a Potato Clock." Retrieved November 25, 2013 (http://www.wikihow.com/Make-a-Potato-Clock).

Zax, David. "The Most Influential Women in Technology 2011—Limor Fried." *Fast Company*. Retrieved November 25, 2013 (http://www.fastcompany.com).

ABOUT THE AUTHOR

Don Rauf is a former editor of the e-newsletter *Student Health 101*, which features many cutting-edge interactive elements and videos. He also authored *Killer Lipstick and Other Spy Gadgets*; *Perry Chen, Yancey Strickler, Charles Adler, and Kickstarter*; and *A Teen's Guide to the Power of Social Networking*. His father was an electrical engineer at IBM, and he dedicates this book to him.

PHOTO CREDITS

Cover, p.1 © iStockphoto.com/roelofse; pp. 4–5, 42 © Arduino; pp. 7, 14, 19, 26, 33, 38, 45, 50 © iStockphoto.com/luxxtek; pp. 8, 12, 22, 27, 28, 34, 51 c.d. stone; p. 11 David Cuartielles/Arduino; p. 15 Mitch Altman/flickr.com/photos/maltman23/5355300305/CC BY-SA 2.0; p. 20 Hack Manhattan; p. 39 © Graham Richter; p. 43 © Pleasant Software; p. 46 Jay Miley; p. 48 Brian Ach/Getty Images; p. 54 © TechShop; interior page design elements © iStockphoto.com/klenger (wires), © iStockphoto.com/A-Digit (circuit board design), © iStockphoto.com/Steven van Soldt (metal plate), © iStockphoto.com/Storman (background pp. 4–5).

Designer: Nelson Sá; Editor: Nicholas Croce;
Photo Researcher: Marty Levick